AF411723

JESSICA BARAN

EQUIVALENTS

Cover photograph by Gina Alvarez
Book design by Ramona Todoca

This book is partially funded by the Wyoming Council on the Arts.

ISBN 978-0-918786-58-6

LOST ROADS PRESS
Post Office Box 146
Kelly, Wyoming 83011

JESSICA BARAN
EQUIVALENTS

The 2012 Besmilr Brigham Women Writers Award

The Besmilr Brigham Award was established in 2012 to commemorate Brigham's work, and to champion work by female writers. The Brigham Award supports female poets beyond the coasts of the U.S. while celebrating Brigham's commitment to the art of writing.

CONTENTS

ACKNOWLEDGEMENTS

It is a great honor to have been selected by poets Danielle Pafunda, Prageeta Sharma, and Susan Scarlata for the inaugural Besmilr Brigham Women Writer's Prize. Immense thanks for their sensitive readership and editorial insight.

Many thanks to the editors of the following journals, where these poems were initially published:

Sink Review: "On Dailiness," 6 & 8
BOMB Magazine: "On Dailiness," 1–5, 7, 9–18
Weekday: "On Dissonance," 1–2, 4, 6, 8, 10, 15, 18–19, 21–24, 27, 30
Harp & Altar: "On Dissonance," 3, 5, 7, 9, 11, 14, 16, 26, 28, 29

Special thanks to Elysia Mann and Steven Brien of All Along Press for creating the illustrated, limited-edition letterpress chapbook, *Late and Soon, Getting and Spending: Prose Sonnets on Dailiness*, in which all of "On Dailiness" first appeared.

Versions of the poems included in "On Dissonance" and "The Panorama" were first written as part of the collaborative project *366 Skies*, with artists Gina Alvarez and Amy Thompson.

Enormous gratitude to my husband and family for their continual support, as well as to Mary Jo Bang, Jennifer Kronovet and Eric Lundgren—who additionally offered invaluable editorial guidance.

ON DAILINESS

1

I'm not interested in propaganda. The space where you arrived is empty when you leave.
The lake is open to questioning. Everyone has a different method: of lending, of accruing
debt. Water can be boiled in all sorts of weather, but the pot cannot be outsourced.
No one thought to peer through a window, as distress was simple. A freight train in the
night. You never thought you'd see the day, but it came. Guilt was no longer deranging.
Language had become flabby. No one had been minding their words. Everyone was
eager to get the point and move forward. No more ruminative wallowing in unclarity.
The bow pulled back, the arrow straight. When you speak your mind, the mind feels
empty. It's been so long since you lived in the present tense. The windows are obscured
by cardboard. The message is bold and indelibly scrawled. It says something like this.

2

"In a time of waste and glut on every front, compression and economy have undeniable appeal." "What is marginalized can also become a form of dissent."

3

Totally normal. The normal. A better brand of inevitability offering a sure thing of uncertainty. Something to stand by, a good method. The kind of stuff that fills afternoons: unlit entryways, central air, bargain prices. Lateral mobility. You're not meant for that kind of direction. Your floor rustles with resilient life. Pestilence is a superior mode of survival. The least desirable things have nothing to give, and it does them well. The most desirable things have everything to take, and it does them well, too. Somewhere in between, in the soft, daily middle: everything that is effortlessly expendable. It's there and then it's gone, and it never has to leave a note.

4

Potential is terrible. Remove better judgment. The muffling capacity of sheets,
how they offer that dream of speechlessness. A tan leather sofa next to a card table
with wheels. The worth of inappropriate behavior. The comforter makes a bed
of sponge-print blossoms—nature in all seasons, poly-blend. An anthem to dailiness.
An American history of lost civility; the decline of small gestures. Cities of the
century in drive-by ruins. Is this the clearing you were looking for? It's not what
you expected: not the rich black burnt thatch long lost woodsmen cleared in a wood
of pines. Not the tractor-flattened part of the meal-colored prairie. Just a carpet
sample thrown on faux terrazzo tiles. Its presence suggests that you curl up like a
penitent preschooler, and nap hard.

5

How did it get this easy? Risk business, risk society. There's no one out there anymore who's a legitimate fool. Information is large and readily informative, and your will is healthy and limitless. We've been misreading, which may be the only way to read. Trivia time. Leisure sports, leisure knowledge, leisure pets. How old we've suddenly become. How angry our pets have gotten. All those trophies of exploit, the mantle gross cluttered. Bring me the better salt, the more conspicuous consumables. Pathologies that sparkle. Why go away when you can see it all here?

6

We all seek to use the skills we have but which too often go unidentified.
Left unattended, or, even worse, misapplied, the world erupts in violence.
Sleep the day away. Too much activity causes impotence. A calendar full
of the husks of purpose. Tear the pages off, use them as fuel. Everything
works much better when less is uttered. There's just so much to avoid.
The swaddled newborn stroking the leopard, the bear nosing the bison:
all mute creatures getting along, making a natural go of it.

7

Let those be the truer difficulties: the pleasure of your company, permissions
given and received. A not-needing-to-know when to stop. Foolish articulations
are not to be regretted but re-edited. Say them again, just better this time. There
are many varieties of jars to fill, so much time on our hands. Whose clock is
ticking—the other fellow's, you hope. Certain jottings, notes on decay. Where to
put the recyclables? It all made it into the correct trash bin. Everyone labored
to make the perfect match. There was a ceiling above, and a basement below.
It's okay. You're making sense. The particulars needn't be devoured. Marvel at all
that hasn't been discussed, at the other person's willful choice to care. Anomalies
stave off anonymity. Plus, you always have the right to change your mind.

8

A man on all fours gives a piggy-back ride to his smaller self. Big Mickey Mouse-gloves
make up the embrace of Father. The four-poster bed where a color-tabbed book and
painter's palette lie; the adjoining twin bed where a mash of flesh vaguely copulates.
The dinner dishes slide off the table, while the table is swallowed by the earth. So many
crossbows and hanging dead game—so little of it will be cooked and eaten. Where have
all the women gone? The enormous, blue-coated man slumps his shoulders, folds his
chained hands. He will allow the Lilliputians to force him to read, though his gaze strays
from the page. The little man at his back gazing watchfully into the obscure distance.
The bones are shoved into the wheelbarrow, as dusk falls in ominous reds. Who will
come through the blackened doorway? What makes them halt, mid-lunge? All the tiny
flags of personal country he grips determinedly in his fists, his legs spread and roped
onto planks. Neither he nor his paint cans are going anywhere. The little yellow flame
coldly bursts in the distance.

9

The anxiety of correspondence — that a letter written and sent will actually arrive. Tough telling. No one thing will invite you to right every wrong. The weather report and the food you eat is a plainer way of getting through the day. It evens out the percentages. The neighbor, too, burns his leaves without conscience.

10

The anxiety of affluence. Distress logs, video loops, the lost trip to Canada.
We reviewed the camping notes. A rainbow appeared in an oil slick; its lack
of shape seemed democratic. Unforced pleasure is difficult to be consistent
about. The sky is a kind of debt. You will be reimbursed. There will be a very
beautiful day after tomorrow. Look at the enormous dishevelment of nighttime
stars and put them into animal order. You found yourself looking. You hold
yourself to be self-evident but still find more to say. The boss says nothing.
I march to the beat of liberty. As long as I love you I am not free. Fuck destiny.
A dream within a dream. What are you, a mind reader? They looked to me
like men who had been somewhere. Committed to error. Expansive in life-lists.
Everything a daily chore. *Stick to your guns* is what somebody yells. Then, in a
whisper, *incidental scrap can make a delicate yield.*

11

Rage versus loneliness. The truer way for clothes to fit. Can you carry history on your
back? There are many moments poised to be photographed but left immemorial. They
clutter obscure storehouses of small worth. In getting back to the basics, sometimes
the argument unspools. The emergency kit contained a bottle for holy water. The bottle
was as empty as a shell. You heard music and it rang through the corridors of the
tall-storied building. What does it mean to have your presence thoroughly fill the air?
Stitch up the holes, become better mended. You expand and contract. Your body is
never of a piece. Feel your own fingers. Sit there, don't offend anyone. July's strawberries
have long since been spilled. All gross-out tactics prove futile. No one has time to look.

12

The vision is comforting: the whole family's getting together to erect a blue tarp
full of holes. It will protect the back-yard TV sets and the small army of portable grills.
We're all saving up for something, a kind of life we see in others that looks desirable,
feels not quite so much when enacted. Only the plumber seems not at a loss for
words. Everyone's house is a little dreamscape. An elf by the wind chime by the faux
vintage sign proclaiming *beach*. Wishful thinking made manifest; the utilities long since
unpaid. Neighbors disdain other neighbors' ways of living. Everyone sees something
flickering through windows at night that looks like the classic bad example. The pile
of chairs, significant waste, the ash tray that reads *better next time*.

13

The battle for another's attention can become a study of cross purposes. You always
wondered what that meant. The letters continued to arrive, full of good consul,
but you nonetheless felt unsated. What anonymous others continually exited in the
night? The building packed with doors, tightly clustered selves. Another mailbox.
An extermination point. All the usual motives for ambition. A collection of salient
endings, moral lessons, context without exposition. Which one was yours among them?

14

The miracle of Maytag. There's no comparison to potted plants. Obsessional hoarding
breeds security, keeps you running from place to place. The burden of reticence.
What does silence strive for? The project has been identified; it's called: *please listen to me.*
What is the nature of your time — considerate, sportive?

15

It was more or less a wash—white walls, white tiles, something foaming at the mouth
that could only be heard, not seen.

16

News passes. I actually think you do know how it goes. Having peered deeply into certain graphic identities, the discarded black plastic bag was finally put to good use. You wondered who would observe that the bag wasn't something you provided. What I'd wanted to say was unavailable to my mouth. But I could hear you. The reddening of hands. The pile of papers by the bed. A reminder: the dog sleeps. The same as usual. The crumpled summons to think beyond the twitching limbs on the floor to being a constituted part. A part of. Something. The delicate and deeper-funneling layers of reproach for every nuance of indiscretion. A flame licks forever on your heels. Be good to yourself. Success is a kind of incivility.

17

The impression was fixed, a common calling sparrow between farther-flung thoughts. We used ourselves primarily—as canvas, medium and interlocutor. An exquisite collection of short-wound clocks. What remained to be written? The true story of hard campaigning. Never fearing combat, the waves of new bodies approaching, filling our now-distantly traipsed black prints. The glory days, over—the field suddenly ugly with snapped stalks. When it occurred, we never stopped blinking.

18

History is cyclical: long lost letters from the past read like something written yesterday, marginal drawings are continued despite the long winding coil of rope. But it draws on, in the face of duplicity; the kids dance anyway. Despite the wearying landscape: tumbledown warehouses, trash-strewn fields, the rusted-out hulk of other buses. The littler monuments crumbling. Almost everything turning cleanly to white. Almost beautiful, this desolation, this fine house. Reoccurring dialogue, often too garbled to decipher, emanates from the plaster-patched walls. In the back room, on a funereal black table strewn with untied ribbons, booklets lay open for perusal: piece-meal installments of a noirish story, torquing between the great and the mundanely abused, the wind-swept highway and the end of all demons. Nothing leading to nothing: the prize-winning plot.

ON DISSONANCE

1

In the first photographs of clouds, a subject never appears. Cloud is simply form—sky without horizon. No buildings, no telephone lines. Over a year's worth, there are more than four hundred of them. Occasionally, poplars appear. The sky nearly black, the sun mostly absent. Special privileges are never granted. Orientation is matterless, making you think less about nature. Everyone at some point looks up.

2

Who did it, you wondered. A mottled mass that went from ash to white. A stretch on the meaning of provisional, meaning something intentionally undone, as the essay better explained. But in this case, more impoverished terms seem fit—how it is that someone else was studying failure so closely, seeing also its productive side.

3

A woman died in a bed next to yours. Starved herself in the night. The next morning,
slowly trudging limp circles around a gymnasium, we tried our best not to over-exert
ourselves. You watched as they penciled in a regimen. Not for her but for you.
Comedy hour—a pile of noontime sitcoms on VHS. Everyone gets together to watch.
Approved normalcy, like the smell of medicinal swabs, wiped-down stainless steel.
Pet the therapy dog, hand-make moccasins. There are right and wrong kinds of abrasion.
You take a moment to consider where to place yourself.

4

Non-objective artwork risks being discussed in terms of the sublime. Sure, you contemplate it. A certain hue is an ecstatic supernova. Layered textures mark brazen leaps. It's all too readily a matter of belief. For you, it's an admirable tidiness. Even belief pays attention to placement. Wind and its compulsion to move, moves you nowhere. Rather, it asserts itself. You love its shallowness. It strips down the metaphor of trying to see.

5

Coming-of-age is a film starring Germany. The blond actor zips up his letterman jacket, aligns his collar with his chin. Walking slowly on the highway outlining the valley's ridge, construction crews can be heard devouring the hillside. He thinks; he says very little. Industry encroaches on nature—a great Modernist trope. You don't disagree. This is the 70s. He arches his eyebrows, and you always say too much. This makes you resemble a great character less. Growing-up happened over three decades ago, sometime before you were born.

6

Not pictures of a lake. No tree line discernible. A gulf between atomized vapor and its thinner, denser self. No cul-de-sac, no drive-way. A no place. Something torn thrown on the floor like a newspaper article, a coupon for discount tools. It looked like forgetting—bright around the periphery. To be stripped again, but of memory this time—you know the shape of it. You like how it resembles nothing you've known before.

7

You once worked at a celebrity hotel. Red couches, white linens, native flourishes.
Loft-style Japanese minimalism in decor. Remember those times as good: mojitos
and sashimi, Paris Hilton stooping to tie her stiletto, Harrison Ford worrying over the
rescue of every wife. One day. Crossing police barricades to enter; your manager
wearing a cloth mask. How can I help you? The British director offered a limo ride.
The Canadian watched from the reception alcove. 10 p.m., 21 years old. The sound
of ice clinking on crystal is a kind of alarm clock other people listen for.

8

Telling this story is easy. Directives and disclosures—all a matter of small differences.

9

Important life event; emotional rupture. Documenting versus fabricating our stories. You heard it on the radio: "The perfect directive for our times: self-curate or vanish." Fabrication can come in the form of organization and selection: pile all of your stuff together in a massive heap and then sort it into more stylish parts. Red bricks with red helmets; yellow cups with yellow kerchiefs. Shit with merde. As you read this, someone is curating their bedside table. Someone is curating their lunch. Someone had something terrible happen to them, once, or twice, in childhood. It provokes little scrutiny until it's placed in the right pile and looks good next to blue. Blue book with blue drawer with big blue watery bottle, like a planet rendered plastic and inflatable and floating lightly across your floor. It and something terrible goes with the twelve other globes.

10

Getting back to the black-out that's really the sky. Where is it going—this vast space, this dark unknowing? Take a closer look—keep track of its behavior. Like an orbiting moon, a weird dumb star, a clever military maneuver you only know from board games. Place doesn't matter any more. Somewhere it's raining, elsewhere it's safe. The difference between what you can grasp in terms of a "greater world view," as the experts say, is not a problem. The big black book, as it now seems, flaps open in the wind. You close the window and promise to worry about it later.

11

Your autobiography is less interesting than when you read or hear about similar
life-events taking place in other peoples' lives. You see it in a coloring book. You see
it in a flea market photo album. You see it on the movie screen, and it strikes you
as authentic. That never happened to you. The color of the sky was raw. You wandered
beneath it, on the narrow shell-strewn beach, at the ridge of a high bluff, looking
for no one in the unrelenting Mediterranean sun of the Antonioni film. It makes for
a palpable memory—that empty sunburn, that cinematic light.

12

A plain, unvarnished impression leaves a burning sensation—a serious inflammation that actually burns a hole through the apparatus. Punctum. This is the language of explication: a collection of occasional terms. Humidity so dense it forms a cottony mantel; a striated rash erupting in air. It's a blemish on distance, an improbable affliction on perspective.

13

Expressions of condolence empty into a paper cake box and fill it with the nothingness they are. To hand that box to its intended recipient is to hand them something much lighter than it should be. It's not the right surprise, unless you're allergic to sugar or dairy, and even then you'd expect something else instead. Expressions of sympathy vary only slightly from condolences as they require a similar but different sized box. More like the kind of box long-stemmed roses arrive in: long and narrow, suggesting elegance over exuberance. Which is right for the occasion? Black balloons, black streamers—it's hateful, you know it; it's all grotesque. What kind of personal feeling led you to believe this was right? Shhhh. Do you hear it? Shhhh, again. It's a rabbit. It runs across the night.

14

Here are a few things you might not notice: a thin wire bent and pressed to the wall, resembling a pencil mark. A wine stain. A house key. You were sick, and a fever raged and broke twice in the night. In the morning: coffee again, mixed with cream and sugar. No more hotels, no more sensate planets. The still life, instead, depicted lunch. And you held your chin in your hand like that, glancing out the window, pretending not to hear when your name was called.

15

Bodies of society look one and the same. It's the difference between the man and his bunny mask. The decision came after increasingly desperate calls. World leaders bristled; dogs brayed. Street festivals lost their usefulness.

16

The picture just wants to be kissed; it's not interested in your feelings. See it bulging from the TV set—balloon-like, glossy lipped. The kind of adult who, after work, mixes a cocktail, retires to the darkroom. He takes artful pictures of what he sees in his life, what he'd like to kiss, maybe. A large black cat, the new gift shop employee. Remember the picture in the museum, the one considered by the protagonist of the last novel you read. It was hanging in the Prado in Madrid. You've been to Madrid but you don't remember visiting the Prado. You did, though, visit your museum in town. There, an exhibit of pictures making real life look like a series of theater sets. You'd taken a picture that looked like one of the pictures in the show, but less massive, less dramatic. It was a picture of your real life, which has nothing to do with museums. Where you're from looks like a place to be driven through irritably; this is how you see it. Light on gravel, light on a window sill. Light lends an abstract quality, and abstraction feels pacific. Downstairs, in the living room, you hear the channels change, and the wind roars like a zoo panther.

17

An era the scale of a day. A pocket-sized wooden yard stick. Looking back doesn't
always look long. These are the local impossibilities—flattening thought into pavement,
recording the viscous tactility of wetness as it amasses on a lens.

18

You killed your hamster. Its name was Baby. You stole coins from your parents' coin jar and confessed this to your parish priest. At the first confession ceremony, the priest told the parish of your theft in his sermon. You got drunk young and had sex late. You lied about being sick. You met many celebrities. You learned quite a lot about confession, visiting therapists for many years. You had lovers in many countries. None of them loved you back. You once took a one-way flight to Toronto. You watched the towers burn. You bought a very expensive black coat. You didn't have a story, but you saw how they worked. A beginning for an ending. Another perceptual fallacy.

19

Outline of light carving diaphanous nothing. The pictures, while luminous, mostly resembled soot. A record of a type of water, and never needing to be accountable. One person's fantasy for language is sexual, the other is existential. Which is yours? It's kind of like the phrase, "you had to be there." No, you didn't. You can check the books later to see how it all adds up.

20

The sky means less when it infers a message. Either way: living with symbols is no surrogate. It's an unspecified reference. Like a photograph, which loses itself in its lack of evidence. It tells you repeatedly the wrong time.

21

Black wash over graveled gray grain. This one looks like it was clawed. A rash of white puffs in a dark expanse is reptilian in texture but not very fast moving.

22

Call it a void. The sea, the lack of sea, the highway periphery's expanse of crops,
the forced announcements that tell you anywhere is actually anywhere else.
You live here. A blank map charting air, dark as a closed closet.

23

It's never easy getting words to work: a bucket is a bucket. Fill it with something.
Set it on the floor—a gallery floor. Suddenly art, it begs for new materials,
other media in which to express itself more clearly. Transparent polymer. Maybe
too proud if reproduced outright—so, let it sag a little. Let it wilt, like a leaf
and not a bucket. This was someone else's problem, you knew, but it struck you
as something worth picking up. Heavy with portent, a shroud of nerve-fibers acting
sensitive, a definite sign.

24

Documenting vs. abstracting our stories. Follow the plot till it falls down a well.
There: where you always unlearn how to speak. Nothing hypnotic—no electrified
soil, mysterious footage or silken rope ladders. Girl Friday loved less for her wit.
Rendering a reflection smudgy, partially erased. "Atmospheric," is what they call it,
like a good hotel lobby. Sure, you might have been there. The well is the lobby.
You sit in a big red couch and wait until your name is called.

25

Pinpricks of time passing. The Fischer Price carnival spins and spins, its Weeble-people drunk on frozen smiles. Vexation is a slow video loop. The coconut continues to hit your head, as you lay stranded under palms on the desert island. Why don't you take off your shoes this time—unfurl your colonial wig. The sky is calling for you—dive in, dive in. Always, a blazing, proverbial ocean.

26

Decades collapse. The wall of VHS cassette tapes does something similar. Somewhere, a piece of A/V equipment is buried, one that plays all the old media and can still attach to your TV. City buses choke past your window; a group of kids pantomime club dancing in a mirror-glass storefront window. Sirens, sounding like big toys, twirl in the distance.

27

Yesterday's Watergate is today's artisanal grain. Don't worry about the details — they don't add up. Such is the case with disjunction: sometimes it takes you along, other times it leaves you. Today is like today: a mixed message. News came in, but it was all too large. And what memory resurrected also looked too obvious. An all-red suit, custom-made. A hoof for the dog to chew on.

28

Q-tips and dental floss, your files of old Post-It notes, trivial likes and even less consequential dislikes. You track the disposal habits of squirrels. Charts analyze the rate of exchange of vinyl for digital. Someone's terribly ill: you discovered it in the dataset. Consumption levels are off, but there's faith in that desire for quantification: you are what you organize. You read yourself in a list.

29

Change is good. The new electrons are looming. A launch is planned this weekend.
Legal services are a burden, but it's a burden to be shared by taxpayers. Do you know
anything about the loan system? Stop and frisk. Realism is for realists. Fundamentalism
comes in many colors. Influence is an industry you're fortunately not qualified for.
You're encouraged by the headlines. There is a cure for this, this hurt. The private sector
now has space to retire to. Like a small crying animal, these slacks should be taken in.

30

Spurred by the idea of progress, that it's a straight-arrow line to an end—that end being where Rome resides, a gold city, or Kansas—you scraped off the filth. Clearing the way is what you thought you were doing, but instead you simply polished a mirror. There you are again. Clouds rush by behind you.

THE PANORAMA

1

Viewers flocked to stand
under the skylight. There: the observation platform,
offering optimal lighting for experiencing

the Great Panorama. There:
the Mississippi lurched, strange
sculpted colossi rose

from its waters, native wars
erupted on surrounding land.
You may say it's vulgar,

but you're wrong.
There's something to see here
in this vast mural. Slave labor

and eviscerated mounds. Memories
of the future, when movies
had yet to exist.

2

Nothing prior to it in history
accounted for the panorama.
It emerged

unlike other forms: out of an urge
for déjà vu. You would look at the great painting
and think, "I've been here before."

And that's
what people wanted:
to be absent and present at once.

3

Popular media. Dioramas, cosmoramas,
Europorama. Either they were too large to move
or too small to consume. Which

is your preferred world view? Daylight.
A subtler peepshow. A means of getting
from soldier to treasure.

The old tower of Babel
from the painting you love
resembles this newer painting,

also exhumed from another time.
There: a burial mound cut in half
like a layer cake,

the inside revealing strata of bones.
The last scene, the one you adore most,
is unfinished. Leaves bristle

around its lower edges,
a half-rendered trunk
of a tree grows.

But it goes nowhere,
the canvas opening up
to white like an entryway, all of it

feeling like a dark tracking shot
in a noir thriller. The camera follows
a hallway until it terminates

at a too-bright bare bulb.
What is there is too washed-out
to discern. Could be gold

or terror—you don't know,
but it seems
like the only direction.

4

The history of certain earth tones
begins with the large midland river—
recalling, alternately, the early landscape tradition

and 70s macramé. It's a history of waiting rooms,
a history of tchotchkes. Ancient scuffles
and situation comedies, alike.

Paintings of it reek of deep storage
and tell the story of where you are from.
Something non-avant-garde,

a dull realism. A clutch of men in bright suits
and white hair carving up waves
on wooden ships.

Colonial postures—knees ceremoniously bent,
arms stretched to conquer or angled
in gloating salute. The postures of the past:

amicable swingers and a preference
for burnt umber decor. A time
of vigorous flag-waving.

The meandering little waves
depicted in outsized white strokes
carry a wrong kind of logic—

you follow it carefully
and can see it clearly
from a distance,

but a break-down occurs
when you get too close.
A white thread

in brown-green linen curtains;
a white latch-hook loop amid Garfield's
orange fur.

A diffuse grid
of soil, water
and grass.

5

A craving for height—a way
of being able to look
down. No longer

was the focal point
the distant, saturated ridge
of stained-glass clerestory windows,

the church spire
dwindling into haze, the menacing gargoyle
and obscure patterns of clouds.

Those spectacles belittled you;
contemplating what's above
indicates you're somewhere below.

This was what
the panorama rectified:
it inverted the view.

Conspicuous consumption
can come in the form of experience:
a craving for sea-sickness, a desire

for apprehension. To boast
of having toured Versailles
versus knowing it by heart.

6

Auroras of history, where the old narratives
dim. Desiccated and mummified bodies,
the ancient burial places,

the magnificent effects of crystallization.
Seeing it as a scene makes it a reality—
dabbed-in with obvious brushwork, a theater

backdrop more tactile than life.
This is what we know of it:
no return is possible. The opulent dessert

-colored skies, the bone of human folly
as it appears post-battle: it's not obvious
where the mark of the hand begins

and ends. Framed like a picture,
it gives you a view
then takes it away.

NOTES

The title of this book, EQUIVALENTS, is borrowed from a suite of photographs
of the sky taken by Alfred Stieglitz between 1925 and 1934.

"The Panorama" evokes the last remaining (panoramic) painting of the Mississippi River
Valley by artist John J. Egan. Around 1850 it was commissioned by amateur archeologist
Dr. Montroville W. Dickeson, and is now in the permanent collection of the Saint
Louis Art Museum.

On Dailiness #10: The lines, *"I march to the beat of liberty. As long as I love you I am
not free,"* are re-interpretations of the title of a 2007 visual art piece by Sharon Hayes.